Puzzle Play
Unicorn mystery

written & illustrated
by Kia Marie Hunt

Published by Collins
An imprint of HarperCollins Publishers
HarperCollins Publishers
Westerhill Road
Bishopbriggs
Glasgow G64 2QT

www.harpercollins.co.uk

HarperCollins Publishers
Macken House,
39/40 Mayor Street Upper,
Dublin 1, Ireland
D01 C9W8

10 9 8 7 6 5 4 3 2 1

ISBN 978-0-00-866593-7

Printed and bound in India

Publisher: Michelle I'Anson
Author and Illustrator: Kia Marie Hunt
Project Manager: Sarah Woods
Designer: Kevin Robbins

Puzzle Play

Unicorn mystery

written & illustrated
by Kia Marie Hunt

Can you solve the Unicorn mystery?

In a big game of hide and seek, Bo the rainbow-horned unicorn is missing! Will you search these magical lands for Bo and help solve this unicorn mystery?

Explore the Ultraviolet Woods and beyond.
Play with unicorns, solve fun Puzzles
and collect clues along the way!

Things you'll need:

- This book
- Some pens, pencils or crayons
- Your amazing brain

That's it!

(You can colour in any bits of this book!)

Always look out for this arrow:

This means you've found a **clue**.

Write down all the clues you find on Page 38.

Your journey begins with Star the unicorn.
Star lives in the Ultraviolet Woods,
where the Light Trees grow.

Can you spot six differences between these two
pictures of Star? Put a circle around each one.

Follow the numbers up each Light Tree and work out the number patterns. Write the missing numbers into the empty circles at the top.

12
16
20
24

4
7
10
13

19
14
9
4

h=🎀 i=♥ l=☁ o=🌀 s=✦ x=✳ e=⭐

Use the pictures in the key above to fill in the missing letters and complete Star's message.

I think I saw Bo! I'll tell you

w __ __ r __ if you f __ __ __
  🎀 ⭐   ⭐   ♥ ✳

my t __ __ __ __ c __ P __ ...
     ⭐ ☁ ⭐ ✦   🌀   ⭐

When you see an arrow like this, write the letter it is pointing to in the key on page 38.

To fix it, find the blue shape that matches the yellow shape and draw a circle around it.

8

Star is a star-gazing unicorn.
She loves to look up at the night sky,
studying the planets (and the stars!).

Can you find the six words
below in the wordsearch?

Words may be hidden across or down.

```
b t w i n k l e
h z a r i y s s
m o o n g e k t
s a k p h b y a
n r i u t d f r
j p l a n e t s
```

moon   night   planets

sky   stars   twinkle

Thanks for fixing my telescope. Let's star-gaze together!

Every green star group has a matching pair, except one. Can you find and circle the odd one out?

How many planets can you see?

If you add up all the numbers in the **purple stars**, what number do you get?

If you add up all the numbers in the **blue stars**, what number do you get?

Can you add colour and patterns to the white stars and planets?

1

5

6

4

3

11

Where did Star last see Bo?

Complete the number problem below each letter. Use the answers to fill in the gaps in the sentence. For example, the number 3 = the letter I.

a
5−4
=

g
2+2
=

l
6−3
=3

n
6+2
=

o
10−3
=

r
6+3
=

s
4+2
=

t
7−2
=

y
7−5
=

I think I saw Bo swimming in the

C _ _ _ _ _ l
9 2 6 5 1 3

L _ _ _ _ _
1 4 7 7 8

Is that Bo's rainbow horn sticking
up out of the water?

You'll have to get closer to find out!

Which path will take you all the way
to the water? Write your answer
(**a**, **b**, **c**, **d** or **e**) in this box:

That's not Bo the unicorn, that's a narwhal!

Use the pictures in the key below
to fill in the missing letters and
complete the narwhal's message.

Some letters have been done for you.

a = ✳   e = ☁   k = ♡   m = ⬡

n = 🕉   p = ✦   r = ⬤   s = ★

Hi there!

My **n** _ _ _ is
🕉 ✳ ⬡ ☁

s _ _ _ _ !
★ ✦ ✳ ⬤ ♡

14

This narwhal lives in the Crystal Lagoon,
where colourful gemstones and crystals float
on the water, sparkling in the sun.

Each gemstone has a matching pair, except one.
Can you find and circle the odd one out?

Colour in the white gems. They are a pair so make them match!

Spark likes to collect crystal shells.
So far, Spark has collected a ruby shell,
an emerald shell, an opal shell and a sapphire shell.

1 **2** **3** **4**

The numbers show the order of a repeating
pattern of shells. Can you complete the line to
the finish? You can only move up, down or sideways.

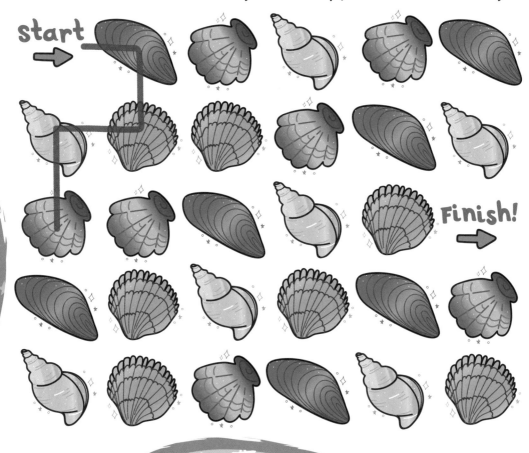

start

Finish!

I'll tell you where I last saw Bo if you help me find a diamond shell for my collection!

Colour in Spark!

To help find a diamond shell for Spark's collection, make your way through the shell maze all the way to the Mermaid Unicorn's Shell Shop.

Start

Finish!

The Mermaid Unicorn's Shell Shop

Welcome to my Shell Shop!

Use the number key to complete the sums below. One has been done for you.

1   2   3   4   5

🐚 + 🐚 + 🐚 = 10

🐚 + 🐚 + 🐚 = ☐

🐚 + 🐚 + 🐚 = ☐

🐚 + 🐚 + 🐚 = ☐

🐚 + 🐚 + 🐚 = ☐

Draw the other half of this shell, then colour it all in.

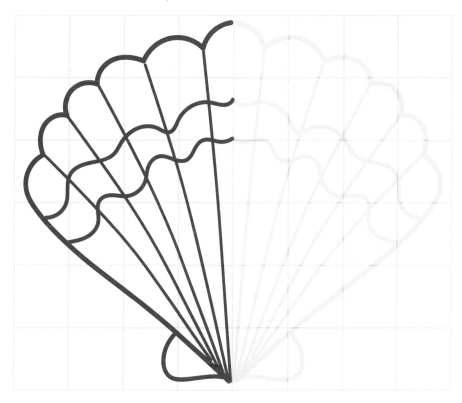

Draw a circle around the purple shape which matches the shape of this special diamond shell.

Can you cross out each letter **z** and write the letters left over onto the lines below to find out where Spark last saw Bo? Some words have been done for you.

sIzthzzinzkzzI

zszazwzBozizn

zzthzzez

zczazzvzezsz

I think _ _ _

_ _ _   _ _   _

_ _ _   _ _ _ _ .

Is that Bo hiding?
You're about to find out!

Which path will take you all the way
to the cave? Write your answer
(**a**, **b**, **c**, or **d**) in this box:

You've found another unicorn, but it's not Bo, it's Glimmer!

Hey, my name is Glimmer!

Make your way through the unicorn maze from start to finish.

start

Finish!

Glimmer's favourite place to play is in the Neon Caves.

Can you spot six differences between these two pictures of the caves? Draw a circle around each one.

Hidden inside the Neon Caves,
there is a room full of bright lights
and fun games to play!

Can you find the six words
below in the wordsearch?

Words may be hidden across or down.

b	g	h	t	a	r	w	l
r	a	z	c	a	q	e	i
i	m	v	a	c	l	k	g
g	e	a	v	f	u	n	h
h	s	t	e	i	j	u	t
t	m	u	s	i	c	d	s

bright   caves   fun

games   lights   music

3 LETTERS:
win

4 LETTERS:
Play

5 LETTERS:
prize
token

6 LETTERS:
bright
ticket

P

b

t

Can you complete the grid with the words above?

Each word is used just once, so cross it off when you place it to help you keep track!

Let's play some games!

Can you use the number key to complete the sums below?

◇ 1   ← 3   → 5   ★ 6

← + ★ + ◇ = ☐

→ + → + ← = ☐

★ + ← + ★ = ☐

Follow the numbers along the line of shapes and work out the number pattern.

Write the missing numbers into the circles.

3

6

9

12

18

21

27

33

39

Draw a circle around the shape that does not have a matching pair!

26

Glimmer will tell you where she saw Bo if you help her win the prize she really wants: a toy unicorn!

Which game claw is picking up the toy unicorn? Write your answer (**a**, **b**, **c** or **d**) in this box:

100 TICKETS

Colour in the other prizes!

Where did Glimmer last see Bo?

Complete the number problem below each letter.
Use the answers to fill in the gaps in the sentence.
For example, the number **4** = the letter **t**.

a
$8-3$
=

g
$2+1$
=

h
$5-3$
=

i
$10-4$
=

n
$6+5$
=

o
$3+5$
=

s
$4+6$
=

t
$8-4$
$= 4$

u
$5-4$
=

I think I saw Bo
galloping over the

L _ _ _ t
  6 3 2 4

M _ _ _ t _ _ _ _
  8 1 11 4 5 6 11 10

It's time to leave the Neon Caves and carry on with your adventure.

To get out, you can only go through the caves with even numbers on them.

You can only move up, down or sideways.

start →

2	6	24	8	3
17	9	5	15	22	13
6	28	2	11	4	20
4	3	24	9	7	6
26	13	22	8	2	28
8	15	7	5	19	17
20	6	4	24	8	Finish! →

Make your way through the maze to the
Light Mountains in the middle.

There, you'll find a strange new creature!

a=▲ c=★ e=⊗ h=✳ m=☁ n=๑ o=✦ t=♡

Hello! I'm B _ _ _ _ _ ,
⊗ ▲ ★ ✦ ๑

I'm a rare-horned
_ _ _ _ _ _ _ !
☁ ▲ ☁ ☁ ✦ ♡ ✳

Use the pictures in the key above to fill in the missing letters and find out who this is.

Colour me in!

31

I saw Bo just a few moments ago! I'll tell you where if you help me light my lanterns...

How many lanterns can you count on this page?

Colour in the white lanterns until there are:
3 pink lanterns
2 blue lanterns
3 purple lanterns
2 orange lanterns
1 black lantern

Which lantern matches the shape of this black lantern? Draw a circle around it.

32

Beacon loves lanterns and is very happy with you for lighting them all!

Can you find the six words below in the wordsearch?

Words may be hidden across or down.

```
e f k q r i n y
f l a n t e r n
i a d r e t y g
r m t o r c h l
e e c a r n d o
c a n d l e x w
```

candle   flame   fire

glow   lantern   torch

Beacon saw Bo only a few moments ago,
so you must be getting close now!

Can you cross out each letter **q** and
write the letters left over onto the lines
below to find out where Beacon saw Bo?
Some words have been done for you.

qIqsqaqqqwqBqoq
qsqqpqlqaqsqhiqnqg
qiqnqtqqhqeq
qwaqqtqerfqalqlq

I saw Bo

_ _ _ _ _ _ _ _ _

_ _ _ _ _

_ _ _ _ _ _ _ _ !

Draw a path on the map to see where you have visited so far and where you are going now:

1 Go **East 3 squares** from **Start**
2 Go **South 2 squares** to the **bridge** and cross it
3 Go **West 2 squares** to the **Crystal Lagoon**
4 Go **South 3 squares**
5 Go **East 2 squares** to the **Neon Caves**
6 Go **North 2 squares** to the **Light Mountains**
7 Go **East 3 squares** to the **bridge** and cross it
8 Go **South 2 squares** to **Finish**

Wow, a rainbow waterfall! The perfect place for a rainbow-horned unicorn to hide!

Can you follow the numbers down the waterfall and work out the number pattern?

Write the missing numbers into the white circles.

2

6

14

18

26

a = 1   e = 2   k = 3   l = 4   p = 5   r = 6   s = 7

Use the pictures in the key above to fill in the missing letters and find out the name of this magical place.

S _ _ _ _ _ _
  5   1   6   3   4   2

F _ _ _ _
  1   4   4   7

Yay! You found Bo the rainbow-horned unicorn!

Join the dots to complete the picture of Bo, then colour it in... Bo loves to be colourful!

Crack the code for a special message...

Look back through the book and collect any letters that have this arrow pointing to them:

These are your clue letters!

Write the missing clue letters into the key below. (For example, because you found the letter 'e' on page 8, the letter 'e' is in the '8' box.)

e
8

12

21

25

28

34

Once your key is ready, you can use it to fill in the missing letters and reveal our special message!

w_ll d_ne, you
  8   25

s_lv_d our u___orn
 25 8   12 28 21

myst__y! We had l_ts
      8 34   25

of fu_ play__g with
      12   28 12

you. Y_u'_e the b_st
       25 34   8

f____d a unic___
34 28 8 12   25 34 12

could w_sh f_r.
        28   25

C_me ba_k soon!
 25   21

Congratulations! Don't forget to complete your Puzzle Play certificate on Page 47!

Answers

Page 6

Page 7

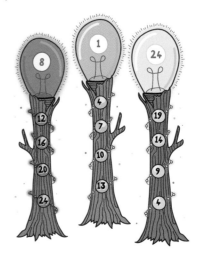

Page 8

To fix it, find the blue shape that matches the yellow shape and put a circle around it.

Page 9

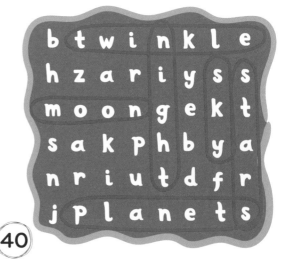

Pages 10 & 11

Every green star group has a matching pair, except one. Can you find and circle the odd one out?

If you add up all the numbers in the purple stars, what number do you get? **12**

If you add up all the numbers in the blue stars, what number do you get? **10**

How many planets can you see? **8**

Page 12

a	g	l	n	o
5-4	2+2	6-3	6+2	10-3
=1	=4	=3	=8	=7

r	s	t	y
6+3	4+2	7-2	7-5
=9	=6	=5	=2

I think I saw Bo swimming in the

C r y s t a l
9 2 6 5 1 3

L a g o o n
1 4 7 7 8

Page 13

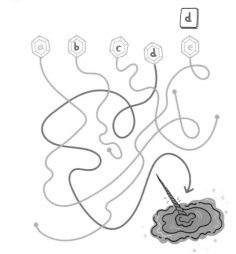

Page 14

Hi there!

My **n a m e** is
9 ✳ ⬡ ☁

S p a r k !
★ ✦ ✳ ● ♡

Page 15

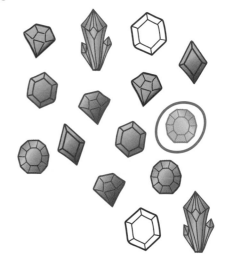

Page 16

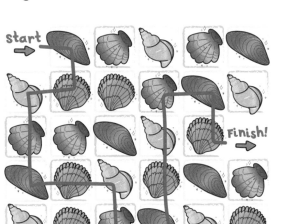

Page 17

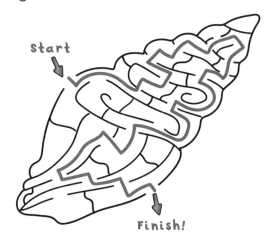

Page 18

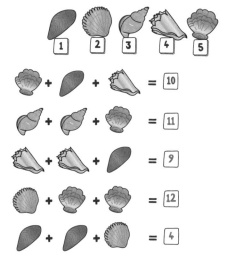

Page 19

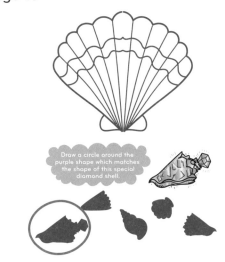

Page 20

Page 21

Page 22

Page 23

Page 24

Page 25

Page 26

Page 27

43

Page 28

a	g	h	i	n
8-3	2+1	5-3	10-4	6+5
= 5	= 3	= 2	= 6	= 11

o	s	t	u
3+5	4+6	8-4	5-4
= 8	= 10	= 4	= 1

I think I saw Bo galloping over the

L i g h t
6 3 2 4

Mo u n t a i n s
8 1 11 4 5 6 11 10

Page 29

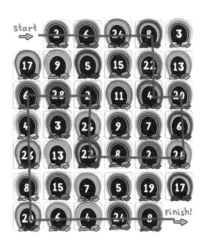

Page 30

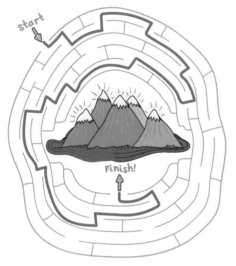

Page 31

Hello! I'm B e a c o n,

I'm a rare horned

m a m m o t h !

Page 32

How many lanterns can you count on this page? **11**

Can you find the lantern that matches the shape of this black lantern? Put a circle around it.

Page 33

e f k q r i n y
f l a n t e r n
i a d r e t y g
r m t o r c h l
e e c a r n d o
c a n d l e x w

I saw Bo splashing in the waterfall!

Sparkle
5 1 6 3 4 2

Falls
1 4 4 7

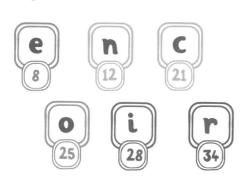

e 8   n 12   c 21
o 25   i 28   r 34

Well done, you
8   25
solved our unicorn
25   8   12 28 21
mystery! We had lots
8 34   25
of fun playing with
12   28 12
you. You're the best
25   34   8
friend a unicorn
34 28 8 12   25 34 12
could wish for.
28   25
Come back soon!
25   21

45

Well done!

This certificate is awarded to:

_____
(your name)

for completing their magical

Puzzle Play

adventure and solving the
unicorn mystery on:

_____
(the date)

_____
(your signature)

Star   Spark   Glimmer   Beacon   Bo